SIENA
THE TOWN HALL
AND CIVIC MUSEUM

A GUIDE-BOOK
TO THE MONUMENTAL BUILDINGS

---

40 illustrations in colour

D0048331

TEXT ALDO CAIROLA
ex Director of the
Civic Museum of Siena

(revised in 1985
by Mauro Civai
present Director
of the Civic Museum)

I.F.I. EDITIONS - Florence

Cover: A. Lorenzetti
The effect of the Good Government on the country:
Nobles hunting.

PRINTED IN ITALY
ALL RIGHTS RESERVED
FOTOCOLOR I.F.I. and GRASSI (Siena)

Campo Square and the Town Hall Palace

Piazza del Campo is not only the center of the city but it is also its spirit. In this square the structure of the city is linked together in an exceptional vision of high level urban planning in a limited space. It is an environment of exceptional beauty in which history and the consequent modification of the buildings, made in a functional and harmonious way, left an indelible mark.

The close weaving of narrow streets suddenly open onto Piazza del Campo where the majestic stone-brick Palace of the Town Hall (pag. 10) closes the square, together with the soaring tower, in an idealistic prospective vision. Any one of the eleven narrow streets nearby leads into the square. The streets themselves conserve their ancient names which gives them an integral part of their original character.

The ample paving of humble brickwork follows the sloping square itself and accentuates the warm earth colors of Siena.

The palaces reveal their past and show the changes they have undergone throughout the centuries; some of the towers have been modified, lowered in most cases, recalling the wealth and power of the past centuries. The essential form of the square which is cloak, fan, or shell shaped, is not so by accident, neither are the nine white bands of stonework which break the rhythm of the red brick paving reminding us of the government of Nine. The Palace and Tower dominate the entire town and time seems to have stopped in a rigorous classical architectural form.

One is reminded of the numerous historical events witnessed by these stone, rock, and brick structures which alternate between the severe essential forms of Gothic architecture and Baroque organic forms which adorn the city and give it its life pulse and many traditions which have been deeply felt and which still live today in the symbol of the Palio. In about the middle of the 13th century, where the Town Hall is now located, there was a sloping hill; rain water ran through the square and was collected in a reservoir of the Old Market next to the square where the first nucleus of the city administration buildings were constructed: the main building was called «Customs» and had storage rooms for communal use, mainly for the storage of salt and the mint. The entire complex of this group of buildings brought about a radical transformation of the nearby area; plans were made to create gutters and drainage systems for water run-off and, at the same time, to give an aesthetic appearance to the new area.

The City Administration began to be an important civic power in the city but lacked an office for its meetings which were still being held in the church of S. Virgilio and S. Cristoforo or in the homes of the local magistrates. With the assembly of 1288 an adjudication was passed regarding land next to the Customs building (the mayor and town council had already established their offices in the Town Hall) where several houses were purchased and, in 1297, a commission was nominated which was composed of twelve members who were entrusted with the responsibility of supervising and planning the project.

Initially, it seems that the former constructions were enlarged; the phase of building of the new Palace should probably be dated between 1297 and 1298. There is some doubt also about the author of the project.

The first building phase regards the central part as, very probably, the Palace was constructed in two different cycles, one following the other; the lower part of the Palace was layed with stone but the upper was of fine brick masonry up to the summit. Parallel to this, work was taking place in the back of the Palace.

It was immediately evident that the high tower could not resolve the problems of the Town Hall and the question was such that soon new work was undertaken to make the wings of the building larger. The right part must have been terminated within 1307 (it was already being used by the Podestà) as the left wing was built to harmonize with the right one in which the other public officials would have their offices.

Around 1310, after making the wings larger, the facade of the Palace appeared in this way: ten Sienese gothic arched doorways adorned with stone ashlars; ten three-mullioned windows of fired brick-work facing the doors of the first floor; on the second floor three mullioned windows, similar to those of the lower floor and in the same perpendicular position; on the third floor three two mullioned windows with crenellated top; on the angle to the left is a vaulting cell bell tower with an alarm bell.

In 1325, nine rooms were added to make the palace liveable and functional. This was modified with the addition of two doors and two three-mullioned windows altering the perfect harmony of the pre-existing structure.

Around this time expansion of the prison was started which was added onto a part of the new wing.

Then, in about 1330, a decision was taken to

add still another floor to the Palace in order to adequately organize the central office of the Council Chamber of the Republic. The work for this part (which faces via Salicotto) was finished in 1342. It was decorated and painted by several painters. Unfortunately, the rectangular plan of the building — similar to that of the Town Hall — and to which it is still joined, did not follow the original structure; in fact, it was remodelled to serve as a theater based on an original design by Riccio. After two disastrous fires in the years 1442-1751, it was rebuilt in 1753 following the plan of Antonio Bibbiena. The offices of the Town Hall are located on the ground floor and today are the main offices of the Civic Theater (entrance from the courtyard of the Town Hall).

But let us return to the Palace and its facade, the modifications and additions of which regard its structure as well as aesthetic changes according to the taste of the time. The following description of changes will give the reader an idea of what was said.

The coat of armas of the viscount — figure of the water snake — was located in the central part (1402) and later substituted (1425) with a large bernardine monogram still to be seen in its original place. In 1560, the coat of arms of the Medici was put between the two coat of arms of the Town.

The granite column and the gilt she-wolf with offspring by Giovanni and Lorenzo of Turino (pag. 11) (the original to be found in the entrance of the

11

monumental halls), was moved from the right to left side in 1549.

In 1680 the second floor was built making the Palace larger on the right side; three mullioned windows were also added, thus, by making a comparison with the photographic documents of the last century, it is evident that there have been considerable alterations from the original aspect. The facade of the Palace has been restored in two different periods as we see it today. Around 1900, a vaulting cell bell tower was built on the right corner in symmetry with the other. In 1904 still other changes were made.

The Tower of Mangia

As it has already been mentioned, in 1325 the equilibrium of the palace facade had been altered because of the great changes of the right hand side.

With the construction of the Tower and Chapel on the outside of the building (pag. 15) a concept different from the severe plastic forms of the mediaeval time was added through the original use of vertical lines, thus giving an original sweeping rhythm to the entire structure. The Tower also became a concrete symbol of a growing political supremacy and flourishing economic equilibrium which contributed significantly to the total development of a well ordered urban plan for the entire town.

The date indicating the beginning of the construction of the Tower is somewhat doubtful since not all of the art historians agree on it; however, it should coincide with the enlarging of the right hand side (1325); the past records show that the work was begun later (1338) and continued until 1349.

We could make a hypothesis that 1338 marked the making of the Tower higher since all of the preceding work was only a preliminary to that which was to follow.

Regarding the people who were involved in this immense undertaking, it seems important to mention the collaboration of the Muccio brothers or Minuccio, Francesco Rinaldo of Perugia, and Ugolino di Vieri who was one of the most famous artisans of jewelry making in Perugia in the early part of the fourteenth century.

Another important consideration is that, when the work on the tower was already in an advanced stage, it was thought it should be different from the other towers and a better suited top was built on it.

The commission to design the top was given to Master Lippo; there is some uncertainty as to whether it was Master Lippo Memmi or Lippo Vanni. One thing is sure, the top, or crown, gives an exceptional architectural value to the tower.

On the long, thin surface of red bricks, suddenly emerges a light, graceful cornice and a large row of merlons supported by four slender arches with four merlons. The belfry rises on it supported by a narrow stand with three merlons on each side. The sienese she-Wolves rains spouts are an added artistic functional element which complete the total harmony.

During the epidemic of bubonic plague in 1348 many plans were cancelled (among them was the construction of the New Cathedral) however, the work around the tower continued without interruption and in 1348 Ricciardo di Tingo was commissioned to cast a bell weighing 17,777 pounds, in substitution of the one which came from Grosseto many years before. The new one was called the «Great Bell» and was used until 1633 when this latter one was substituted with a bell cast by the master caster Antonio Ceramini of Novara. This undertaking was not completed and only after ten years — in 1644 — a decision was taken to make still another bell commissioned to two master casters, Girolamo Santoni from Fano and Gio. Battista Salvini from Siena; the new bell was installed in 1665. It was called «Sunto» after the name of Maria Assunta. It is known as «Campanone» (Big Bell) weighing 6,764 kilos. The height of the tower, including the metal scaffolding which supports the bell, is 102 meters.

The panorama which one can enjoy from the top of the Tower merits a description: the severity of the urban planning of the Town is to be discovered through the thick network of narrow streets full of closely nestled roof-tops. The Piazza del Campo looks like a fan enhanced by the handsome form of the Fountain. Then the great white structures of the Cathedral of S. Domenico and the Servi, then the defense wall of the Town and the countryside, which is filled with lovely little valleys extending as far as the eye can see into the horizon until earth and sky meet in a fusion of clear blue. The landscape becomes a living part of the town history representing a unique example of town-country planning.

As the town made different uses of the Tower (as watch tower, also used to warn people in time of danger, as a watch to detect fires, to call for urgent meetings, or just to tell the time), it is important to recall the history of the clocks which marked the history of the Tower.

Initially, the duty of striking the exact hour was entrusted to the pages of the Town Hall; in 1347 the head bell ringer was Giovanni Balduccio who, for his wasteful habits regarding money, was nick-named «mangiaguadagi» or spendthrift or, more simply, «Mangia» (waster). The name of the Tower came from this nickname which was, however, jus-tified by the fact that the Town Administration of the local government had to bear heavy expenses in order to keep the clock functioning.

The first mechanism entered into service in 1360; later it was repaired in 1379, then successive-ly remade by Don Guasparre of the Ubaldini. An automaton which chimed the hours was later added.

This new device was given the name of the «old bell ringer». The first automaton was made of wood; in 1665 — after having been restored several times — it was replaced with one of stone, remade in 1759 in travertine. It was then removed from the Tower in 1780 and its parts, put back together, are now to be seen in the courtyard of the Podestà. From 1780 the hours were chimed by a bronze hammer; the mechanism was overhauled in 1804 by Giovan Lorenzo Barbetti.

Around the clock, Maestro Martino and his son Jacopo della Quercia, painted the so-called «mostra dell'orologio». Then, in 1776, Angelo Bini created a flowing cornice in white marble which was ornamented by Carlo Amidei; other previous painters who had worked on this «Mostra» were Alessandro Casolini and Bernardino Mei.

The Chapel of Campo

The chapel was built at the base of the Tower to fulfill a vow made during the epidemic of bubonic plague in 1348. In 1352, Domenico d'Agostino began this project; later the chapel suffered altering which changed its original architectural order. Antonio Federighi restored the chapel according to its original plan of 1376 and finished it in 1468, giving to it its present-day form in which we can see the beautiful classic freeze of fighting griffins.

This brought to the filling up of the last two two-mullioned windows on the first floor of the Palace, thus completing the work which was begun a long time before with the purpose of integrating the Palace, the Tower, and the Chapel, into a harmonious architectural order.

In this way, a rather successful harmonization was reached between the renaissance element contrasting with the predominant gothic character of the various buildings.

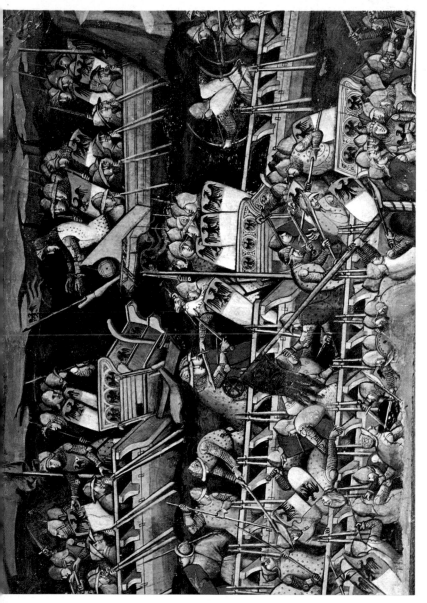

The six statues, sculpted between 1377 and 1422 (which are standing in their predisposed niches) from the right are: S. Giacomo Maggiore, by Bartolomeo di Tomme; S. Giacomo Minore, by Lando di Stefano; S. Bartolommeo (1382), by Lando di Stefano; S. Giovanni Battista, by Lando di Stefano; S. Pietro, by Bartolommeo di Tomme; S. Tommaso, by Giovanni di Turino.

The lateral parapets come from previous constructions and the front ones, attributed to Federighi «allegorie dell'Aritmetica e della Geometria» (allegory of Mathematics and Geometry), were replaced by copies done by Enea Becheroni in 1848. The original sections are installed on the stairway of the Town Hall.

The wrought iron gate is the creation of Conte di Lelio Orlandi and Petruccio di Betto (15th century).

The fresco of the altar depicting «la Madonna con Santi» (Madonna with Saints), (1537-38) by Giovanni Antonio Bazzi called Sodoma, was removed for restoration during which a precious sinopia was discovered and is now on exhibition in the Picture Gallery of the Civic Museum.

The halls of the main floor

The whole ground floor is for office use and meeting halls and therefore, not open to the public. A summarized guide outline is available to give some hints about the interesting history of this area.

In 1680, C. Battista Piccolomini transformed the courtyard passageway of the Palace by constructing a stairway to the upper floors and giving to this side the aspect it has today (right hand side on entering).

The pillasters of brick construction and portions of the supporting arches can still be seen. The symmetry of this courtyard is comparable to that of the Podestà (the last of which was restored to its original architectural form in 1931 by Architect Chierici.

As soon as one enters the door which still has its original antique wings, one sees two bronze tablets in memory of the pebliscite for the annexation of Tuscany (1860), the other represents the news bulletin of the victory of the first world war.

26

By following the stairway and then entering through the ample paned glass doorway, one enters into the monumental halls, civic museum, and hall of representatives.

Entrance Hall.

On the left wall, the «lupe senesi» (the she-wolves of Siena) are attributed to the school of Giovanni Pisano; between the two wolves, «Mosè fa scaturire l'acqua» (Moses makes the water gush), by Antonio Federighi, previously part of the fountain of the old ghetto.

First hall to the left.

Formerly it was the chapel of the Palace (then substituted by the one next to the «Sala del Mappamondo» 'World Map Hall'): on the ceiling of this chapel is a fresco depicting «Cristo Benedicente» (Christ Blessing), recently attributed to the last period of activity of Simone Martini in Siena, «i quattro Evangelisti» (The Four Evangelists); on the wall in front of the window fragments of «Annunciazione» (Annunciation); the other frescoes are «S.

Antonio Abate» and the «Blessed Andrea Gallerani and Ambrogio Sansedoni» (about 1390) by Bartolo Fredi.

«Lupa senese» (The sienese she-wolf), an example of original artisan work of the 16th century, was greatly changed at the beginning of the 19th cent.

Third hall to the left.

«Ufficio di Assessori Municipali» (Office of the Municipal Aldermen): this fresco was discovered in 1872. It represents the «Madonna della Misericordia» (Madonna of Mercy), a fine example of Sienese Quattrocento by Lorenzo di Pietro called il «Vecchietta».

On the left, high up: «aquila imperiale» (imperial eagle) with spread wings and symbols of the government of Siena, a fresco by Sodoma, under which was the «Resurrezione di Cristo» (Resurrection of Christ) (1535) also by Sodoma, removed in 1842 and transferred to the hall where the Secretary General of the Town Hall has his offices.

All the rooms on the opposite side were used by the Magistrate of Bicchierna in which very interesting names, coats of arms, and inscriptions are to be found.

First room at the end of the entrance hall to the right.

Office of the Secretary General.

Here there is the famous fresco of Sodoma already mentioned.

On the main part of the outside arch leading into the anteroom, is a fresco with «Tre Santi» (Three Saints) (1446) by Sano di Pietro with the magnificent image of Siena.

In the middle hall between the office of the Secretary General and that of the «Sindaco» (Mayor), is the anteroom.

Anteroom.

This hall is completely decorated and frescoed. «L'Incoronazione della Vergine» (The Incoronation of the Vergin) painted in the first and perhaps unfinished version by Lippo Vanni (1352), was painted again in another version by Sano di Pietro (1445) but it is possible that Domenico di Bartoli worked on it too (see figures with bow).

Several painters of Siena contributed to the decoration of the hall towards the end of the 16th and 17th century.

We shall mention: Francesco Nasini: Annunci-

azione della Vergine» (Annunciation of the Virgin)
(1689); «Allegorie Bibliche» (Biblical Allegories)
attributed to Rutilio Manetti; «Allegorie ed episodi
storici» (Allegories and historic episodes) by Ventura Salimbeni (1577-1580); the decoration of the
ceiling is partially to be attributed to Astolfo Petraz-
zi «episodi dei Santi Protettori» (episodes of the
Protecting Saints), the frescoes of the ceiling recalling episodes of the city history, are by an unknown
artist.

Hall of the Mayor.

In the center of the ceiling is an oil painting
representing «presentation of the model of the
monastery of S. Maria» by Domenico Manetti; in
the other panels are works by Alessandro Casolani,
Francesco Nasini and Annibale Mazzuoli.

The decor is completed with a fresco attributed
to Sodoma, «La Madonna, il Bambino, il piccolo S.
Giovanni e Santi» (The Madonna, the Child, S.
Giovanni as a child and saints) (1537); «La Trasla-
zione del Cardinale Petroni» (The removal of Cardinal Petroni) is by Francesco Nasini (1689).

Over the arch of the door are «Quattro putti che
sollevano un drappo» (four angels lifting a drape)
(1560) by Bartolomeo Neroni called «il Riccio»
(the Hedgehog).

34

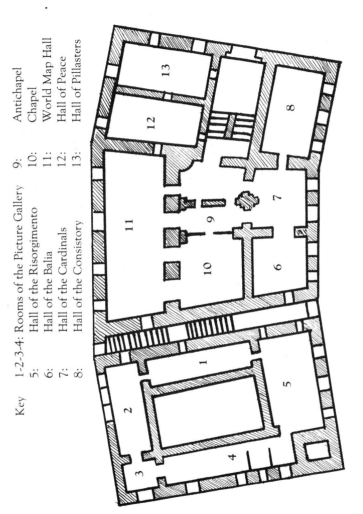

Key   1-2-3-4: Rooms of the Picture Gallery   9:   Antichapel
      5:   Hall of the Risorgimento   10:   Chapel
      6:   Hall of the Balia   11:   World Map Hall
      7:   Hall of the Cardinals   12:   Hall of Peace
      8:   Hall of the Consistory   13:   Hall of Pillasters

Stairway leading to the Civic Museum

A recently restored iron staircase leads from the courtyard of the Podestà to the monumental halls of the Town Hall.

On display on the first landing, along with some large iron chests, there is an antique bell (1109) from the Church of Saint Christopher.

On the upper landing there is a rich series of majolicaware (plates, vases, amphors) prevalently of Sienese production. Most of these relics date back to the 18th century although some pieces are even older.

Halls of the first floor and Civic Museum

The rooms of the Picture Gallery. (1-2-3-4)

In the first room of the Picture Gallery, which has just recently been rearranged, paintings by non-Sienese artists from the 16th, 17th and 18th centuries can be seen. There are four large particularly important *Hunting Scenes* attributed to Rosa da Tivoli, «Tobia che reacquista la vista» (Tobias' sight returning) from the Genoese school of Bernardo Strozzi called «il Cappuccino» and a *Madonna with Child* a work of the Venetian Felice Brusasorzi.

crucifixus etiam pro nobis sub pon
tio pilato

Sienese paintings from the 16th and beginning of the 17th century are on display in the second room of the Picture Gallery. These important Sienese artists include Bartolomeo Neroni. Note the «Cataletto» (a portable bed or stretcher for four people) from the Society of Saint Stephen and a *Crucifixion* by Ventura Salimbeni (1568-1613). The small tablet painting representing the *Stoning of Saint Stephen* is an early work by Francesco Vanni (1563-1610).

The structure in the middle of the room is used for the temporary exhibition of small works belonging to the Commune of Siena which have been restored.

In the following room, the third, there are several paintings from the Sienese school dating back to the 17th century. There is a remarkable series of small genre paintings attributed to Vincenzo Rustici (1577-1632) illustrating the *Months of the Year* and a large *Globe* of French production from the 18th century.

In the fourth room of the Picture Gallery there are numerous Sienese paintings from the 17th and 18th centuries. Here there are some valuable works by Rutilio Manetti (1571-1639): *Saint Paul, The Adoration of the Magi* and *Saint Jerome*, painted when the artist was at his peek.

In the middle of the room is the *Banner of the*

Society of Saint Sebastian by Sebastiano Folli, and a showcase displaying goldsmithry (chalices, reliquary, thurible) note the silver-plated bust of Saint Giles.

Hall of the Risorgimento. (5)

A large number of Sienese artists painted the glorious events of the Risorgimento, between 1886 and 1891, in this vast hall which was once part of the apartments of the Magistrates.

In the center of the ceiling frescoed by Giorgio Bandini, Alessandro Franchi painted «l'Italia tra la Libertà e l'Indipendenza» (Italy between Liberty and Independence) adding to it some lines by Manzoni. The allegories of the Italian regions are painted in the ten corbels of the vault: Sardinia and Liguria, Veneto and Lombardy by Alessandro Franchi; Pied-mont, Calabria and Sicily by Riccardo Meacci; Emilia, Tuscany, Umbria and Marche by Antonio Ridolfi; Lazio, Puglia, Sannio, Campania and Lucania by Gaetano Marinelli.

The six large frescoes on the walls represent: «L'incontro presso Novara tra Vittorio Emanuele II e il Maresciallo Radetzky» (March 14, 1849) by Pietro Aldi (Victor Emanuel 2nd Marshal Radetzky meet near Novara). «Vittorio Emanuele II alla bat-

43

taglia di Palestro» (May 31, 1859) (Victor Emanuel 2nd during the battle of Palestro); «La battaglia di S. Martino» (24th June, 1859) (The battle of Saint Martin) both works by Amos Cassioli; «L'incontro tra il re e Giuseppe Garibaldi» (October 16, 1860) (the meeting of the King and Giuseppe Garibaldi) by Pietro Aldi (pag. 90); «La presentazione dei risultati del plebiscito» (October 9, 1870) and «I funerali di Vittorio Emanuele II al Pantheon» (January 16, 1878) (The results of the plebiscite), (The funeral of Victor Emanuel 2nd at the Pantheon), both by Cesare Maccari.

Paintings and sculpture from the 19th century have been added to this hall recently. The atrists are prevalently Sienese, for example Tito Sarrocchi, Giovanni Duprè, Emilio Gallori (pag. 19) and Luigi Mussini.

This hall leads right to the Tower of Mangia.

Hall of Balia. (6)

In 1445, the Magistrates of Balia used to have their meetings here. The hall is interesting because of its pictorial decorations and also because its architecture reminds one of the adjacent Chapel. A short arch divides it into two parts; it is frescoed by: Spinello Aretino, his son Parri and Martino da Bartolommeo who painted the vaulting cells.

The upper part, painted in 1408, is crossed by diagonal ribs with starred blue backgrounds, freezes, leaves and town coat of arms; in each compartment there is a Virtue with its name (except two which are illegible): «Intelligenza, Prudenza, Sapienza, Umiltà, Castità, Temperanza, Nobiltà, Misericordia, Pace, Giustizia, Continenza, Grazia, Forza, Circospezione» (Intelligence, Prudence, Wisdom, Humility, Chastity, Temperance, Nobility, Mercy, Peace, Justice, Continence, Grace, Strength, Circumspection).

Above the cornice plinth painted in large panels and supported by painted cornice moulding is the «Storia di papa Alessandro III, Rolando Paparoni Bandinelli e della Lega Lombarda» (the story of Pope Alexander 3rd, Rolando Paparoni and the Lombard Alliance), referring in particular to the victory over Federico barbarossa (Frederick the Red-bearded).

The pilasters have a varied decoration, with leaves and panels with coat of arms of the Republic and half figures of emperors and warriors: according to a reliable tradition Goffredo di Buglione is one of them.

On the intrados (arching inner part of the cupolas) in small, cuspidal tabernacles are painted the Evangelists, each one for the corresponding symbolical figure.

Spinello Aretino, with the help of his son Parri,

worked on these frescoes between 1405 and 1407; it must be noted that the post Giottesque design and use of colour of the more important cycle are clearly in contrast with the typically Sienese linear style of Martino di Bartolommeo.

The sequence of the stories of Alexander 3rd is to be read in the following way: wall above the transversal arch, in the lunette: «L'antipapa Vittore IV riveste il manto pontificale» (Vittore 4th, the Antipope, wearing the papal robe); in the other lunette: «Il Papa a Ninfa riconosciuto ed ossequiato» (The people of Ninfa recognize che Pope and pay their respects to him); in the nearby lunette: «L'Incoronazione di Papa Alessandro III» (The coronation of Pope Alexander 3rd) (1159); below: «Il Pontefice consegna la spada al Doge Ziani» (the Pope gives the sword to the Doge Ziani).

On the wall of the entrance door the lunettes represent: «Colloquio tra Alessandro III e il re di Francia Ludovico VIII» (1162) and «Il Papa che esce da Roma, occupata dal Barbarossa, con le vesti di un certosino» (Conversation between Alexander 3rd and the King of France, Ludovico 8th) (The Pope leaving Rome occupied by Frederick the Red-bearded, disguised as a Carthusian monk); below: «La leggendaria battaglia navale dei Veneziani contro gli Imperiali presso Savore» (The famous naval battle of the Venetians against the Imperial forces near Savore) (pag. 23).

In the lunette above the two windows are: «Il messaggio di Federico al Papa» (1174) and «Il perdono del Barbarossa» (The message of Frederick to the Pope) (Frederick the Red-bearded's pardon).

On the wall opposite the entrance we can see: «Il Papa ritorna a Roma» (The Pope's return to Rome) with the Emperor, the Doge Ziani and a long retinue of cardinals and prelates (page 22). In the two lunettes are: «Il Congresso di Vienna» (1177) and «La canonizzazione di S. Canuto, re di Danimarca» and «S. Tommaso, arcivescovo di Canterbury» (The Congress of Vienna) (The canonization of Saint Canute, king of Denmark) (Saint Thomas, archbishop of Canterbury).

On the wall right next to it there is «L'imperatore sdraiato ai piedi del Papa in atto di sottomissione» (The emperor at the foot of the Pope, submitting to him) (the figure of Frederick, the Red-bearded has been altered several times for political reasons); in the above lunette there is: «La fondazione di Alessandria della Paglia» (1168) (The foundation of Alessandria della Paglia).

In the lunette of the transversal arch are depicted: «Sinodo Lateranense III» (1179) and «Il favoloso rogo dei quattro antipapi» (The Lateran Synod) (The four antipopes at the stake) (They were: Ottaviano of the Counts of Tuscolo, Vittore 4th, Guido da Crema, Pasquale 2nd) who, under the rule of Alexander 3rd, went on a schism for as long as 24 years.

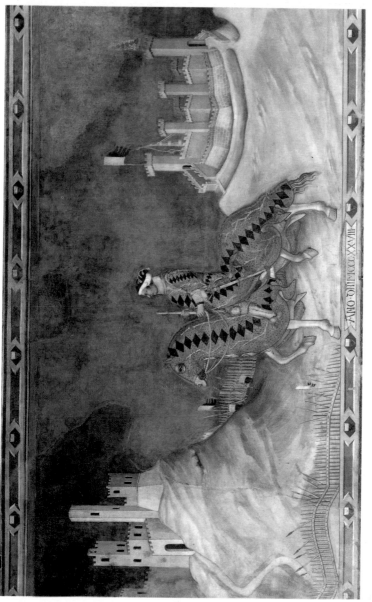

51

The inlaid door leading to the Chapel is by Domenico di Niccolò.

The inlaid piece against the wall with the fresco of the «ritorno del Papa a Roma» (the Pope returning to Rome) is by Barna di Turino (about 1410).

The cycle of works by Spinello is an exception as compared with the other works in the Palace: the main subject is that of the moralising, secular cycles with typical religious scenes (as the celebration of the Virgin and of the patron saints) together with the celebrations of victories taking place in the city. The only exception, but only as to the value of the symbol, is «Guido Riccio». On the contrary, in this case, a non-Sienese painter, extols the deeds of a famous citizen (namely, a Pope), linked to the history of Italy.

Hall of the Cardinals. (7)

The so-called Hall of the Cardinals in a hallway. (Here there were paintings representing the Sienesi Cardinals). The hall was decorated by Giorgio Bandini (end of the 19th cent.). It contains five frescoes some of which are detached.

On the wall facing the window is a «Madonna col Bambino e quattro angeli» (Madonna with Child and four Angels) (1434) painted on a panel with a gilt frame by Matteo di Giovanni (formerly attributed to Cozzarelli) (pag. 26).

Some polychrome wooden statues are on display in this hall, one particularly important one is *Saint Nicholas of Bari* attributed to Antonio Federighi (1423 c.-1490).

In the central showcase there are some carved chests embellished with inlaying, ballot-boxes and other relics used by civil magistrates including the *Commander of the Militia's Pike* (15th century).

Hall of the Concistory (or of the Tapestries). (8)

It is devoted to the memory of the Magistrates who continued ruling the city even after the end of the Republic (1555). An elegant portal (1468) attributed to Bernardo Rossellino leads to the hall; the wooden door is attributed to Domenico Niccolò «dei Cori». The frescoes decorating the vault were painted by Domenico Beccafumi between 1529 and 1535 who used a historical Roman and Greek repertory to extol «episodi di amor patrio» (episodes of love for one's country).

In the center there is the «Allegoria della Giustizia» (Allegory of Justice) painted with a very skilful perspective. Right next to it there are «Concordia» and «Amor di Patria» (Concord and love for one's country) on two octagonal panels. All around this is the story of Marco Pepido and Fulvio Flacco, censors, who were enemies and became friends for the love of their country. There is also the story of

QVELICHI FIORECTI ROSE
CH' D PROPIO STATO DISPREÇA Q

Codro, king of Athens who sacrificed his life so that the prophecy, promising victory to the people whose king would die on the battle field, might come true. Then there is the story of Spurio Cassio who was killed because he wanted to become a tyrant. Marco Manilio's case who was sentenced for the same reason. We can then see the example of Postumio Dittatore who taught his soldiers the importance of obedience giving them the example of this through the death of his son. Here is Publio Muzio, a tribune, who was responsible for having his collegues burned at the stake; we can also see Spurio Melio sentenced to death as he wanted to become a tyrant; there is also Seleuco, Prince of Locri, who had one of his eyes and one of his son's eyes taken out so as not to break the law. In the four corners of the vault are represented eight Greek and Roman heroes, side by side: Trasubulo, Genunzio, Celio, Coronda, Damone, Lucio Bruto, Fabio Massimo, Speusippo.

On the left walls and the back wall there are three Gobelin tapestries, made at the end of the 17th cent., representing the allegories of Earth (pag. 27), Water and Fire, commemorating the reign of Ludovico 14th, formerly in the Uffizi Gallery.

On the other walls there are 17th cent. tapestries woven in the Medici's workshops.

Above the door there is a large painting by Luca Giordano representing «il Giudizio di Salomone» (Solomon's Judgement).

Antichapel and chapel of the Palace. (9-10)

This part of the Palace shows the changes which took place on the interior structure of the building at the beginning of the 15th cent., when the whole ground floor was assigned to the Offices of the Magistrates and the small interior chapel was not used any longer (the ceiling of the chapel was frescoed by Simone Martini). The chapel had been built on order of the Nine right next to the entrance door. On the floor where the Town Authorities were going to live, another chapel was built, which we are now going to describe.

Four large arches connecting the «sacred» area of the World Map Hall were built within 1406, by which date also the adjacent Hall of Balia was finished.

Taddeo di Bartolo was entrusted with the pictorial decoration of the hall, which he accomplished between 1407 and 1414. Below the arch leading to the World Map Hall there is an archeological view of Rome surrounded by Mars, Jupiter, Apollo and Pallas; at the side of the left arch is represented Aristotle, on the right there are Caesar and Pompeus Magnus. Other historical personages of the Republic of Rome are to be seen on the wall facing the Chapel, namely: M.T. Cicero, A. Porcius Cato Uticense, Scipio Nasica, Curio Dentato, M. Furio Camillo, Scipione Africano (inscriptions are next to each name).

A long explanation in caption, points out good examples to be followed by the Rulers of the Republic. The subject of the Good Government, together with a precious documentation of humanistic interest, is again depicted here in connection with the subject of unity tying together the great painting cycles in the Palace.

The figure of S. Cristoforo (Saint Christopher) (pag. 30), stands out on the smaller wall; in the lunettes, at the top are «la Giustizia e la Magnanimità» (Justice and Magnanimity).

On the interior of the arch leading to the anteroom of the Chapel is the image of «Religione» (Religion). Brutus Junior and Lelio are depicted in the squares of the arches; on the pillasters are to be seen Beato Ambrogio and Judas Maccabeus.

A wrought-iron and lead gate separates the vestibule from the Chapel; the design of this valuable, rare example of artistic handicraft, is attributed to Jacopo della Quercia (1414). The workmanship was done by Giacomo di Giovanni di Vito and by his son Giovanni (about 1424) (pag. 31).

The holy water basin supported by two gilt bronze angels (1434) was made with a precious taste for the goldsmith's art, by Giovanni e Lorenzo di Turino; also the «Cristo» (statue of Christ) (1438), in gilt bronze is by Giovanni di Turino.

Opposite the gate is a showcase containing valuable objects of goldsmithry among which is a *Golden Rose* made by Simone of Florence (pag. 34) donated to the town by Pope Pius II in 1458. A 14th century *Peace Treaty* gilded and enamelled with Christ triumphant, the Evangelists and the city coat of arms is on display as well as a *Gothic Chalice* dating back to the 15th century and a *Helmet of the Commander of the Militia* on loan from the Pendola Institute (15th century).

The Chapel is preserved in its original state, except for the altar and the painting on it.

On the choir-stall are depicted the articles of the Creed; a precious work by Domenico di Niccolò «dei Cori» (choir-stall), so-called due to his masterful skill as choir-stall carver. Maestro di Matteo Vanni (pages 35-38-39-42-43) collaborated on the piece, the execution of which took five years (1425-1429).

The marble altar was moved here from the Cathedral in 1686; it was made by Lorenzo Marrina. «La Sacra Famiglia e San Leonardo» (the Holy Family and Saint Leonard) is considered an early work by Sodoma and it also comes from the Siena Cathedral (pag. 46).

In the right corner there is a small organ, made by Maestro Giovanni Piffero and by Ghino d'Antonio (1524).

The frescoes represent «episodi della vita della Vergine» (episodes of the Life of the Virgin), right before and after her death: «Il congedo degli Apostoli, la morte di Maria» (the Apostles take their leave, the death of Mary), «il trasporto della salma, la Assunzione in cielo (Mary's body is being carried away, the Assumption to Heaven) (page 47); on the vault and the sprandels there are «Angeli, Evangelisti e Dottori della Chiesa» (Angels, Evangelists and the Doctors of the Church).

On the squares of the arch, above the gate, there are «I Profeti Eliseo e Corababel e le Virtù Cardinali» (Eliseo and Corababel, the Prophets and the Cardinal Virtues). On the pillasters corresponding to the arches are: «S. Giovanni Battista, S. Agostino, il Beato Giovacchino dei Servi e il Beato Francesco d'Assisi» (Saint John the Baptist, Sain Joachim of the Serfs and the Blessed Francis of Assisi). On the back wall there is the «Annunciazione» (the Annunciation), in a rather bad state or repair.

The vast cycle of Taddeo di Bartolo clearly points out two motifs: a profane and moralising one in the antichapel, the other one being a synthesis of religious subjects already consecrated by tradition; but the two works complete each other and find their right place in the wider treatment of the subject of the alternative between religious and political power (already noted in the World Map Hall).

World Map Hall. (11)

This is the largest hall of the Palace and the one which, in a certain sense, summarizes the historic and artistic events of the Palace. Here, in fact, the «Consiglio» (the Town Council) found its ideal environment. The Town Council had the Chapel near it and next to it the Armory (for crossbow storage) now called «Sala della Pace» (Hall of Peace).

Religious faith in the Virgin, protectress and mother, political and military security; these are the themes which are to be found on the frescoed walls of the hall. «La Maestà» (Majesty) and «Guidoriccio da Fogliano».

The name of the hall was derived «ab antiquo» from a globe, most likely mounted on pivots, which represented the antique territories dominated by the Senesi; the World Map which was in its place until the middle of the 18th century, has been attributed to Ambrogio Lorenzetti and was installed on the lower part of the wall where the Guidoriccio is.

«La Maestà» (Majesty) (pagg. 50-54-55) is the first frescoed work of Simone Martini, painted in 1315, the middle section of which was painted again in the year 1321.

The present condition of the fresco does not

permit a clear vision of it but still shows that this fresco is a great masterpiece of pictorial composition. It symbolizes the spirit of devotion of the people of Siena towards the Virgin in a subtle distinction between a merely religious theme and a non-religious environment. (There are verses regarding this on the steps of the throne in the answer of the Madonna: Dilecti mei ponete nelle menti cho' li devoti preghi onesti / come vorete voi faro' contenti / ma se i potenti a' debili fien molesti, / gravando loro con vergogne o danni / le vostre oration non sono per questi / né per qualunque la sua terra inganni). (Take honest pleasure in meditating and prayer / I will make you happy if you will / but if the powerful molest the weak, / burdening them with taxes, shame, or harm, / your prayers are not for them / or for anyone who deceives the others on this earth).

In the center of the fresco the Madonna is sitting on a rich throne with spires holding little Jesus on her knee; at the foot of the throne two kneeling angels offer baskets of flowers; the Patron Saints of the City are also kneeling; around them are angels, seraphs, the Apostles Peter, Paul, and John, and other saints, such as, Agnes and Mary Magdalene.

The large canopy, with its waving ribbons, gives a fresh vitality to the scene showing the procession which has just stopped.

There is a fresco depicting Guidoriccio da Fogliano on the opposite wall (pag. 51-59) another work by the Sienese master Simone Martini. The date of execution is still in doubt, however, it can be estimated to be after 1328. (This date, which can be seen under the fresco, may refer to the date of the Sienese victory against the warriors of Montemassi and Sassoforte).

The heraldic symbols of the fresco — the horsecloth and clothing of the knight — the bare landscape of the Maremma, the parade pace of the horse, the profile of the knight, the decorative draping of the horsecloth blown by the breeze, the introduction of fortifications and war machines in the landscape, contribute to give an original example of pre-renaissance vision of the «portrait» meant as an expression of «Virtue», underlining a strong military power in which the figure of man becomes the symbol of force of the state.

The fresco below the painting of *Guidoriccio* was recently discovered, older than the painting above, it illustrates *Two People and a Castle* (pag. 62-63).

The discovery of this fresco has created lively debate and an ample series of contrasting attributions among art historians. However, the quality of the painting is excellent and it certainly dates back to before the Trecento-a period of maximum expansionist vivacity for the Sienese Republic.

The most convincing and documented attribution undoubtedly ascribes this work to Duccio di Buoninsegna. The fresco, which illustrates the peaceful cession of Giuncarico's castle to the Commune of Siena in 1314, may well be Duccio's last work of art.

The restoration of the entire frescoed wall has permitted the exposure of deep marks on the wall made by Ambrogio Lorenzetti's *World Map*-a globe with rotating movement.

Two other frescoes painted on the wall are: «S. Vittore» on the right and «S. Ansano» to the left; the images of the two «Patroni» (Patron Saints) are by Giovanni Antonio Bazzi called Sodoma (1529).

On the main wall opposite the window above the large arches, is the figure of S. Paolo armed with a sword near the gate of the city from which angels are existing with crosses and weapons. The composition represents «La battaglia contro la Compagnia del Cappello» (The battle against the Followers of Cappello); the clash took palce in Val di Chiana in 1363.

Following this painting, in which yellow ochre was used as a warm earth color, is the «Vittoria di Poggio imperiale» (Victory of Poggio Imperiale) won by the Sienese near Poggibonsi in 1479. This part of the composition was painted by Giovanni Cristoforo and Francesco d'Andrea.

On the lower pillars: «Blessed Bernardino To-
lomei» (1553) by Sodoma; «S. Bernardino» (1450)
by Sano di Pietro; «S. Caterina da Siena» (1461) by
Lorenzo di Pietro (pag. 66) also called the «Blessed
Andrea Gallerani» followers of Bartolomeo Neroni
nicknamed «il Riccio» (Hedgehog).

On the internal part of the surface of the third
arch which opens onto che Chapel are the saints
«Giovacchino and Francesco»; on the opposite wall
is a bernadinian monogram with the name of Christ.

Hall of Peace (or the Nine). (12)

Called in this way because of the pictoric theme
by Ambrogio Lorenzetti and because the government of the Nine met here. The Nine commissioned
the painter to execute the fresco between 1337 and
1339 with evident reference to the political ideas of
the time. The hall was an arsenal and armory for
crossbows during the past centuries.

«Il buono e il cattivo governo» (The Good and
Bad Government) is about the consequences of the
ruling power in the city and country. These are the
themes which the painter mixed with «filosofia»
(philosophy) and life in an avant-garde painting
unique for its time.

From the analysis of the symbols — antithesis
for good and bad, and the opposing of these in a

precise historic and environmental documentation — we can understand the interlinking of events represented in an exemplary synthesis of the complex «social development», the pulsating life of the city and surrounding countryside thus giving a moral, political, social value to the whole scene.

The basis for this analysis is to be gathered from the allegory of the «Allegorie del Buon Governo» (Good Government) (pag. 67); surrounded by «Virtù Civili» (Civic Virtue) above which there are «Fede, Speranza e Carità» (Faith, Hope and Charity), Symbolized by an old white bearded man dressed in white and black robes sitting on a rich throne and holding a sceptre and seal of the Town of Siena his feet resting on the She-Wolf with the twins nearby.

Around the Good Government are six female figures representing: «Pace, Fortezza, Prudenza, Magnanimità, Temperanza e Giustizia» (Peace, Fortitude, Prudence, Magnanimity, Temperance and Justice) (pag. 70-71). Represented in the lower part of the fresco are, on the right, soldiers walking and on horseback escorting chained prisoners, while on the opposite side is the group of twenty four citizens walking side by side. Almost in the middle part are two noblemen who are offering their castles to the Good Government.

«La Giustizia» (Justice) (pag. 74), which was previously among the allegorical figures, is particularly important, so much so that the painter repeats

74

its motif in the left side representing it as the equilibrating element of balance. «Sapienza» (Knowledge) is right above it. On the right scale-pan is represented «Giustizia Commutativa» (Commutative Justice); on the left scale-pan there is «Giustizia Distributiva» (Distributing Justice). From the two scale-pans hang the ropes held in the right hand by a female figure representing «La Concordia» (Concord) in whose lap there is a plane. The rope is held by the citizens «concordi legati insieme» (in agreement - tied to one another) but the other end of it is held by the Old Man.

On the right wall are depicted the «effetti del Buon Governo nella città e nelle campagne» (effects of good government on the town and country) where there is peace, life flows calmly, the people work hard, trade is flourishing (pag. 75-78-79-82).

The activity of the town is visualized in the intermingled elements of reality and imagination, in which the urbanistic structure reminds one of Siena and its spaces; there is no breaking point between town and country. The synthesis of the territory of Siena includes also agrarian aspects, customs and meditative elements; all the activities of peaceful living are expressed in this fresco which is pervaded by Securitas (secure life).

On the opposite wall, in a bad state of repair, the scene depicted is in contrast with the serenity of peace and good government. The almost animal-like figure in the center represents «Tirannide» (Tyranny) (pag. 83); there are six figures near it (three on each side) namely: «Crudeltà, Inganno, Frode, Furore, Discordia e Perfidia» (Cruelty, Deceit, Fraud, Wrath, Discord and Wickedness); «Giustizia» (Justice) is tied, put in chains and trodden at the foot of the six vices.

On the other side of the wall are depicted the misfortunes caused by wars and civil strife: towns and fields on fire, people arrested, robbed, raped and slaughtered. «Terrore» (Terror) dominates the whole scene. The long captions of the frescoes are particularly interesting also as a help to read the whole cycle.

Hall of the Pillasters. (13)

The next hall is called Sala dei Pilastri (Hall of the Pillasters) (so-called as it was necessary to build pillasters in the hall because of the closing up of some of the loggias in the nearby Malborghetto).

The oldest paintings of the Civic Museum are on display in this hall.

On the right hand wall is a panel painting representing a «Maestà» (Majesty) by Guido da Siena (pag. 86); formerly in the Cathedral of S. Domenico. This painting is a precious testimony of the

beginning of the Sienese school. It has given to historians and critics alike doubts about its dating since the signature and date (MCCXXI) appear to be authentic and therefore the painting by Guido is held to be a copy of a former painting of the same subject which was destroyed; the date being preserved so as to obtain indulgences and privileges connected to the lost work. The picture may be datable between 1275 and 1280.

A remarkable repainting of the face and hands of the *Madonna and Child* during the first years of the 14th century are to be noted. The restoration was done by a follower of Duccio.

Other noteworthy panels on display are the «predica di S. Bernardino in piazza del Campo» (S. Bernardino preaching in piazza del Campo) (1440) by Neroccio di Bartolommeo Landi (pag. 87), an «Annunciazione» (Annunciation) of the Sienese School of the 14th century (pag. 90), a panel with «Madonna e Bambino» (Virgin and Child) by the School of Duccio of the 14th century and a glass window, attributed to Ambrogio Lorenzetti, representing «San Michele Arcangelo che uccide il drago» (St. Michael the Archangel killing the dragon).

In the showcase there are two 14th century chests, one ironshod and the other made of gilded plaster; both are richly decorated.

The collections of the Civic Museum

The coin collection is arranged and properly protected, inside the palace. Permission to see the collection may be obtained on request only for study research. Also the collections of customer credit cards and the medals may be seen on request.

In the third hall there is a wooden cabinet containing part of the collection of seals; the collection consists of three kinds of seals; seals of offices and countries; seals of communities and of ecclesiastical people; seals of citizens. There are sixteen Roman seals, four hundred and twenty pieces up to the 14th and 15th cent. and one hundred and seventy five pieces up to the 19th cent.; it is completed by eight-one anepigraphical pieces, eighteen seal rings, thirty-nine punchers. Another interesting collection of the Civic Museum is that of the prints which were formerly in some of the halls of the second floor of the Palace, right next to the Loggia of the Fonte Gaia.

Loggia of the Gaia Fountain

From the Risorgimento Hall there is a wide staircase leading to the Loggia.

83

Reaching the top of it, on the left side there is another section of the Museum: the gipsotheque.

In the halls are to be found plaster casts (many of which had been shown on the occasion of the exhibition of old Sienese art held in 1904) of works by Agostino and Agnolo di Duccio (1330), by Lorenzo Marrina (1489), by Jacopo della Quercia; reproductions of the relief works for S. Petronio's in Bologna, of the sepulchral monument of Ilaria del Carretto, the bas-relief of Fonte Gaia and plaster casts of Giovanni Duprè.

In the 14th cent., the large loggia at the back of the Palace was raised since more space was needed for the Priors and Officials of the Town Hall as they were compelled to live in the Palace during the two months of their office as Maigstrates and they could not leave the Palace except on special occasions, when public ceremonies were held.

During the above mentioned exhibition of 1904, the parts of the Gaia fountain by Jacopo della Quercia were arranged here. The fountain had been removed from Piazza del Campo in 1868 and was, later on, replaced by a free copy by the Sienese sculptor Tito Sarrocchi. The copy is still in the same place. The work, which is damaged and corroded, is standing next to the three walls of the loggia. The important group was commissioned in 1409 but Jacopo finished it only after about ten years and many vicissitudes and law suits.

On the left wall there is: «La creazione di Adamo»; «La Sapienza»; «La Speranza» (only the head remains); (Adam's Creation), (Knowledge), (Hope). In the large center part there are: «La Fortezza», «La Prudenza», «La Madonna col Bambino e due agnelli», «La Giustizia», «La Carità» (pag. 91); (Fortitude), (Prudence), (Madonna with Child and two lambs), (Justice), (Charity). On the right wall there are: «La Temperanza», «La Fede», «La cacciata di Adamo ed Eva dal Paradiso terrestre»; (Temperance), (Faith), (Adam and Eve chased from Eden). At the opposite sides there are two full-relief statues perhaps of Rea Silvia and Acca Laurenzia, but more probably being allegories of Charity.

The view from the Loggia is varied and splendid; the lovely Valley of Arbia extending as far as the Amiata mountains, the market place with its typical houses, the outstanding apse of St. Agostino's and the densely populated districts of the Contrade of the Onda and of the Torre: a testimonial of the importance of the preservation of the landscape.

Hall of the Condottiere.

A small door to the right leads to the halls containing interesting frescoes. In the first room, in a fine aedicula, are to be admired: «Crucifix»

(1446) by Pietro di Giovanni d'Ambrogio; on the ceiling there are lunettes and coat-of-arms of Condottieri and Magistrates in the 16th and 17th cent.

In the second little room which is the secret antechamber of the Condottiere, on the left wall there is: «View of Piazza del Campo with a procession of knights taking the golden rose to the cathedral». The rose was given by Pope Alexander 7th to the city in 1658. The fresco was done a short time later. On the ceiling there are more coat of arms and names of Condottieri and other members of the group of the Magistrates of the 17th cent.

In the third hall, called the hall of the Condottiere, on the vault there is the symbol of the Republic inside a wreath sculpted in marble; in the lunettes, some of which are in a bad state of repair, there are some tempera works representing religious and non religious episodes of Siena. Perhaps the most important document, at least for what concerns the story of the Palio, is contained in the lunette on the right above the entrance door representing «View of Piazza Grande and procession for the buffalo race». In the lunette on the left of the door there is: «Flaminio del Taia is given the cardinal hat by Pope Innocent 11th». In the first lunette of the right side there is: «The Senesi troops go to the Cathedral with the Magistrate after the battle of

Camollia» (1526). In the second lunette: «Pope Alexander 7th puts the cardinal's hat on his nephew's head». In the vault: «Jesus in the temple». On the left wall in the first lunette there is «Blessed Franco da Grotti restores the eyesight of a blind boy». In the second lunette: «The Magistrate of the city in front of the Madonna of the Vow»; in the third lunette: «Flight to Egypt and Procession to carry the Madonna of Provenzano to the Church dedicated to Her». In the right bottom corner: «The prophet Brandano».

On the ceiling of the third hall the large antechamber of the Condottiere, which was used for particularly important visits, there is «the Virgin amidst the clouds turning a thunderbolt off from its course». The rather unusual subject of this fresco refers to a fact which took place in 1734: the Condottiere Tommaso Petrucci, together with other Magistrates had been saved from a thunderbolt.

On the walls and the ceiling there are coat of arms and inscriptions.

Hall of the Seigniory.

The town hall council meets in this hall.
Several Sienesi painters: Francesco Vanni, Ventura Salimbeni, Pietro Sorri, Sebastiano Folli, Cristoforo e Francesco Rustici, Bernardino Mei worked

90

in this room between the end of the 16th and the beginning of the 17th cent. celebrating the pomp and magnificence of Siena.

The cornice is decorated with a coat of arms indicating the year of the execution of the work and the names of the Magistrates who commissioned it.

In the lunette between the two windows there is: «The Assumption of Mary» between two allegorical figures. Below there is a Medici coat-of-arms, at the right of which there is the Sienese Balzana and at the left of which there is a shield with an eagle against a golden background. Below there is the particular insignia of the Granduke Cosimo 3rd with the arm of his wife, the granduchess.

In the other lunettes are represented the following episodes of the history of Siena: «S. Ambrogio Sansedoni obtains the absolution from Pope Martin 4th for all the Sienesi interdicts» (1596); «The Battle of Radi 1312 won by the Sienesi against Arrigo 7th» (1598); «Saint Catherine in Avignon implores the Pope and the Pope on his way to Rome» (1597). «Pius 2nd shows the Priors the arm of S. John the Baptist which he gave them in 1464» (1592); «The battle of Monteaperti of September 4, 1260» (1597); «Allegories of the benefits granted by Charles 4th in 1351 to the Sienese Studio» (1598); «Antioch conquered by the Sienesi crusaders and Salimbeni patriarch of the city in 1406» (1597); «The Council of 1509 in the Cathedral of Siena and the proclamation of Pope Niccolò 2nd» (1598); «The Sienesi defeat Arrigo 7th near the bridge of Rosario with the help of the Virgin» (1598); «Jesus appears as a leper to Beato Giovanni Colombini and Urban 5th approves the rule of the Jesuits» (1600); «Prayer of young S. Bernard and the saint preaching in Piazza del Campo» (1598); «The Sienesi drive back the troops of Charles 4th in 1368» (1592); «Don Antonio Piccolomini consecrated as the first archbishop of Siena, by Pius 2nd in 1459 is entering the town» (1598); «Victory of the Sienesi over the people of Orvieti near Montepulciano» (1599); «Martyrdom of Saint Ansano, baptist and patron saint of Siena» (1595).

On the walls there are two large pictures by Amos Cassioli (1875): «The oath of Pontida and Provenzan Salvani in the Campo of Siena».

In the antechamber, which can also be reached from the loggia, through the door at the left, there are frescoes in the center of the ceiling representing: «The She-Wolf of Siena with the Balzana»; on the right wall there is a painting by Antonio Nasini dated 1690 with coat of arms of the Condottiere and other Magistrates representing «General Ottavio Piccolomini»; above the door there is: «Ritratto di Vittorio Emanuele II», a picture by Luigi Mussini; above the door leading to the Hall of the Seigniory there is: «Coat of arms with the Balzana and the rampant lion» (1654).

INDEX